Who said

Great?

27 poems for 27 years of life.

RJ Izquierdo

Table of Contents

Dedication

I dedicate this book to Monty and AD. Long live the junkyard.

Acknowledgements

I would like to acknowledge all of you that have taken the time to purchase this book and are actively choosing to be inspired. I would like to encourage you to draw your own illustrations for each poem, hopefully connecting you deeper with the words and giving new insight to everyday conundrums.

About the Author

RJ Izquierdo has expressed himself through many different creative mediums. Growing up in palisades park, New Jersey, RJ has truly made a name for himself and his hometown. This poetry book allows us to take a closer look into the artist's mind and thought process while creating and acting over the past 7 years.

ME

I admire myself.

Not the present version of me.

But the me I know I have the potential to be.

The me that I have seen, again and again,

Go above and beyond.

The me I pray to God,

To give me the strength and wisdom to become.

Nobody's perfect, so I wouldn't want to be like anyone.

I am proud to be my parent's son.

Perspective

As I slip out of this world and begin to enter another, I lose control of my body

It goes limp and lifeless, but my vision transforms. I see endless possibilities and reforms.

I float, and I dream.

I am once again reborn.

Electric lights short circuit my brain.

The hard wiring is rewired into endless possibilities Rather than what could have been.

I see with my own two eyes the prospects of this new world. The opportunities each situation presents.

How every move you make taps into the circuit board of the universe, Engraving your imprint in history.

Mom's Back

I crack

I got so many emotions I'm about to crack. Lotion can't
even help, and these are the facts. I seem to get off track,

After I attract everything, I ever want.

So here I am.

Haunted, flaunted, and taunted. Can't express my thoughts.

"Not that I would ever."

But shit's getting heavy.

I mean, I can do better than Chevy and Belushi.

I'm in it for friends, family, laughs, cheddar, and sushi.

Gone

Where do we go when we know where we want to be and where we need to be?

Who do we want to be with, and who we came with?

Loyalty is something you never question in yourself, even if you betray yourself.

Someone takes the shirt off their back, and you wonder what they want back.

I know where I wanna be and who needs me.

Who feeds me? Who pleases me?

I swear I'm coming. I'm coming.

Because it's what I want and what you need. Pleasing the masses because you're my world.

So if I'm running from you, I'm running from myself. But I'm always there.

So

Am I going or coming again?

1-100

Filed by the moon

I thrive under her darkness.

The rare sight in the day brings me luck in France. A day
away from praise and forever on the rise.

I dance in the morning for mourning.

Play

If life is a game. How do we win?

Ashtray

With each exhale, I astray from reality,

And indulge in the clouds of smoke that portray my life.

The fallacies and fantasies become a temporary reality,

And the opportunities of life are inhaled and evaporated.

With each breath, I gain and lose those dreams. The dreams
I have fabricated and manufactured.

And as another dream is lost, I exhale and begin to go
astray.

Silent Surrender

It is not in my power to swing the flag of surrender. It is not

my right.

I may lay here barren and stripped, before the Gods,

Withered away by

life and its fights.

Begging for defeat.

Yet it is not mine to take

Just as victory is not my entitlement.

The begs and please of millions fall silent.

2 Cents

Looking at these walls, I count 6.

Tell me, what you see,

What do you hear?

What do you fear?

Tell me, do you feel the same when I am near? I just want
to be clear.

I have shed my tears, Tears of joy, tears of pain.

Hopefully, tears of fame.

All because I stayed the same.

I never knew how to be nobody but me.

With In

Where is the help I need?

Turn it off, you can't go back, right on track.

Still wish it could be easier. Clearer? Harder?

Who doesn't love a good challenge? Spit in your hair, cut
up your face.

Gritty and witty.

It is a must for championship glory. Sorry lord, for the
chores

Birds have wings to sore

I wish to be 1 with two 4's. Can't get this thing started, But
we don't say we can't.

So off to dream, we sleep with our memories to delete.

Inner high

Dive deeper than your heart.

Choose to trust and invest. Choose to do your part. Loneliness can come in the most crowded places. Stay true to yourself and put smiles on their faces. Choose to fail in all the best ways.

Go all out and be what you say you're about.

Angel

Untethered to this world,

She subtly navigates through life

Extracting each piece of love and knowledge, Kindness,

and Compassion.

Significant and noteworthy, she is a student of life.

Learning its many lessons and questing for the light That

shines so brightly within her.

WE

You do you, and I'll do me.

But just because we're doing us, doesn't mean we can't be

we.

Forgotten City

Spray-painted City shines bright tonight. In the morning,
we see the fight.

The streets at night with velvet lights. Can't we stay here
forever?

Wouldn't it be Clever, If we had a little plan? I wish I was
your man.

But I take what I can, and I take what I get. Yes, you come,
and you forget.

Bed Time

I felt disconcerting stillness as I drew each breath.

My eyelids began to flutter like the wings of a
hummingbird. I tasted the smile on my face that sat a mile
long.

Green tea leaves floated through my nostrils All the while
The silent growls of the crocodile drew near.

I felt alone, but still, I could feel the growls of the
crocodile.

My Dear Time

My dear,

My biggest fear is wasted time. Wasting mine and wasting yours. Why do this when that is better?

Why waste this on that when that can get me this? You tell me I'm all you want, but what do you want?

A person has needs, and others have lives to live.

You wasting my time is just as much a fear that is controlled by me.

So I waste my time by wasting yours. Goodbye to me and hello to forever with you.

Daily Routine

I'm up at 4

I awake on the floor.

I repeat to myself; I can't do this anymore.

You haunt my dreams. I don't know what it means

I just want to be seen. For once.

One More

One more kiss before you leave, Darling. Another morning
we stare into each other's eyes. Hesitant to say our
goodbyes.

I blink, and you fly. You cry, and I'm high. Never been the
guy, Always the kid.

Excuse the spit. It's just too big.

Please tell me how you fig

That this is finna fit

Bite your lip.

Love your pillow grip. Excuse me, that's just the tip.

Please

Please keep flexing.

I live for that shit.

You and your friends in a bar tee.

My family and I are on the Mediterranean Sea. Let me hear about your weekend getaway, and I'll tell you about the month I got laid. It's different over here,

I don't dream in color, because my life is so vivid. I see into the future, catching you slipping.

Swiss Glory

There is no glory in quick victories.

The restless and hungry shall prosper. Heavily. Pride and

Ego

Will be the greatest of men

DOWN

FALL.

May Wisdom, courage, and strength illuminate

THE WAY.

Hold On

Hold on as long as you can, just a little longer

Okay, set a goal of 10 minutes

No way Ahhhh

Okay, that thought made the time pass

How about another

Just hold on, I'm slipping. Re-grip, Regroup, and keep going. This is better. No, it's not. No, no, no, no

Just a little longer

180

Guilt is only 180

There will always be a source.

When it settles in, the conclusions begin to flash. Where
will this go?

How will it end?

I deserve this.

I'm going to do wrong. The circles in reverse

And I'm stuck in the middle. No matter what you do,

Karma will always come 360.

W

Ask the questions.

What do I want to do? Why do I want to do it? Where do I want to do it?

Who do I want to do it with? Answer all that, and you win.

Destiny's Mystery

Every evening eventually, I feel it in my stomach.

What is this feeling?

I have several ideas.

Is it the feeling I'm not doing enough or

Am I wasting time doing the wrong thing? Is something big

coming?

Is it good or bad?

I know I'm ready for whatever it is Because God made me

this way

But still, I feel that uncertainty in my stomach. A true

mystery.

Every day.

What's meant to be will be, I tell myself.

I do what's right, and everything will be alright. My

destiny is written in the stars.

I'm just going to go read the sky.

Time settles my stomach like ever Tea. I accept my fate,

never my rate.

They owe me more, and it dawns on me.

I got money on my mind and in my stomach. The root of

evil, no wonder I can't stop it.

The reason I feel uneasy? That's no mystery.

Hit My Line

I can't seem to find you.

Call me.

I got what you need.

You've been looking for it, and it's me. There must be a
disconnect.

I planted this seed

I hope that you will contact me

And say the things I've been dying to hear. You got nothing
to fear.

It was all worth it.

You are who you said you were. So now you're validated.

A call or a check. A check or a call. I need something

My phone and I are both low and About to die.

So come and save me, Or just shoot me a text.

Gifts

The energy and intentions given to me are not of a human hand.

The situation and opportunities I am giving cannot simply be manifested. Hours of intent.

Joules of energy.

Sacrificed for a single cause. Until the perfect moment.

When timing meets preparation and you seize it without hesitation.

This was not given, but it was always yours. So thank yourself for being you.

For you being you is the greatest gift you got.

Big Time

Fake lights for a fake show.

The money's real, and so are the feels. But the people

The emotions

The display is fake.

Eat the food; it's not fresh.

Take a picture to capture a false memory

Tell yourself this laughter is the only remedy.

Retail therapy cures what someone said to me

None of this is real though

What do you want? It's already yours.

So move on and get ready for the next project. That's all
they want.

The next thing is because the last ones are gone, and the
next one is a mystery. None of it's real, but it's,

The big time.

CPSIA information can be obtained
at www.ICGtesting.com
Printed in the USA
BVHW030515211122
652410BV00013B/382

9 781088 072271